# WHO'S THE STRONGEST?

BY KIRSTY HOLMES

Please visit our website, www.garethstevens.com. For a free color catalog of all our high-quality books, call toll free 1-800-542-2595 or fax 1-877-542-2596.

Cataloging-in-Publication Data

Names: Holmes, Kirsty.
Title: Who's the strongest? / Kirsty Holmes.
Description: New York: Gareth Stevens Publishing, 2022. | Series: Animal vs. animal | Includes glossary and index.
Identifiers: ISBN 9781534537460 (pbk.) | ISBN 9781534537484 (library bound) | ISBN 9781534537477 (6 pack) | ISBN 9781534537491 (ebook)
Subjects: LCSH: Morphology (Animals)--Juvenile literature. | Animals--Juvenile literature. | Physiology--Juvenile literature.
Classification: LCC QL799.3 H68 2022 | DDC 591.4'1--dc23

Published in 2022 by
**Gareth Stevens Publishing**
29 East 21st Street
New York, NY 10010



Edited by: Robin Twiddy
Designed by: Danielle Rippengill

Printed in the United States of America



CPSIA compliance information: Batch #CSGS22: For further information contact Gareth Stevens, New York, New York at 1-800-542-2595.



## IMAGE CREDITS

*All images are courtesy of Shutterstock.com, unless otherwise specified. With thanks to Getty Images, Thinkstock Photo, and iStockphoto. Cover – Ovocheva, Stepova Oksana, Abscent, Guz Anna, Yevgenij_D. Images used on every page – Ovocheva, Stepova Oksana. 5 – ONYXprj, Abscent. 6 – Guz Anna. 6&7 – Guingm. 8 – Jurgen Vogt. 9 – ricochet64. 8&9 – Guingm. 10&11 – Abscent. 12 – Michael Potter11, Guz Anna. 13 – khlungcenter. 12&13 – Guingm. 14 – Guz Anna. 14&15 – Abscent. 16 – Volodymyr Burdiak. 17 – Giedriius. 16&17 – Guingm. 18&19 – Abscent. 20&21 – amiloslava. 22 – Guingm. 23 – Abscent.*

# CONTENTS



**Words that look like this can be found in the glossary on page 24.**

**Step right up!**

It's the Great and Small Games!

See nature's fiercest and finest creatures in action!

**Today's events:**

The Tree Trunk Lift!

Strong-Bug Circus!

Tug-of-War!

These events will surely decide once and for all:

Who's the Strongest?

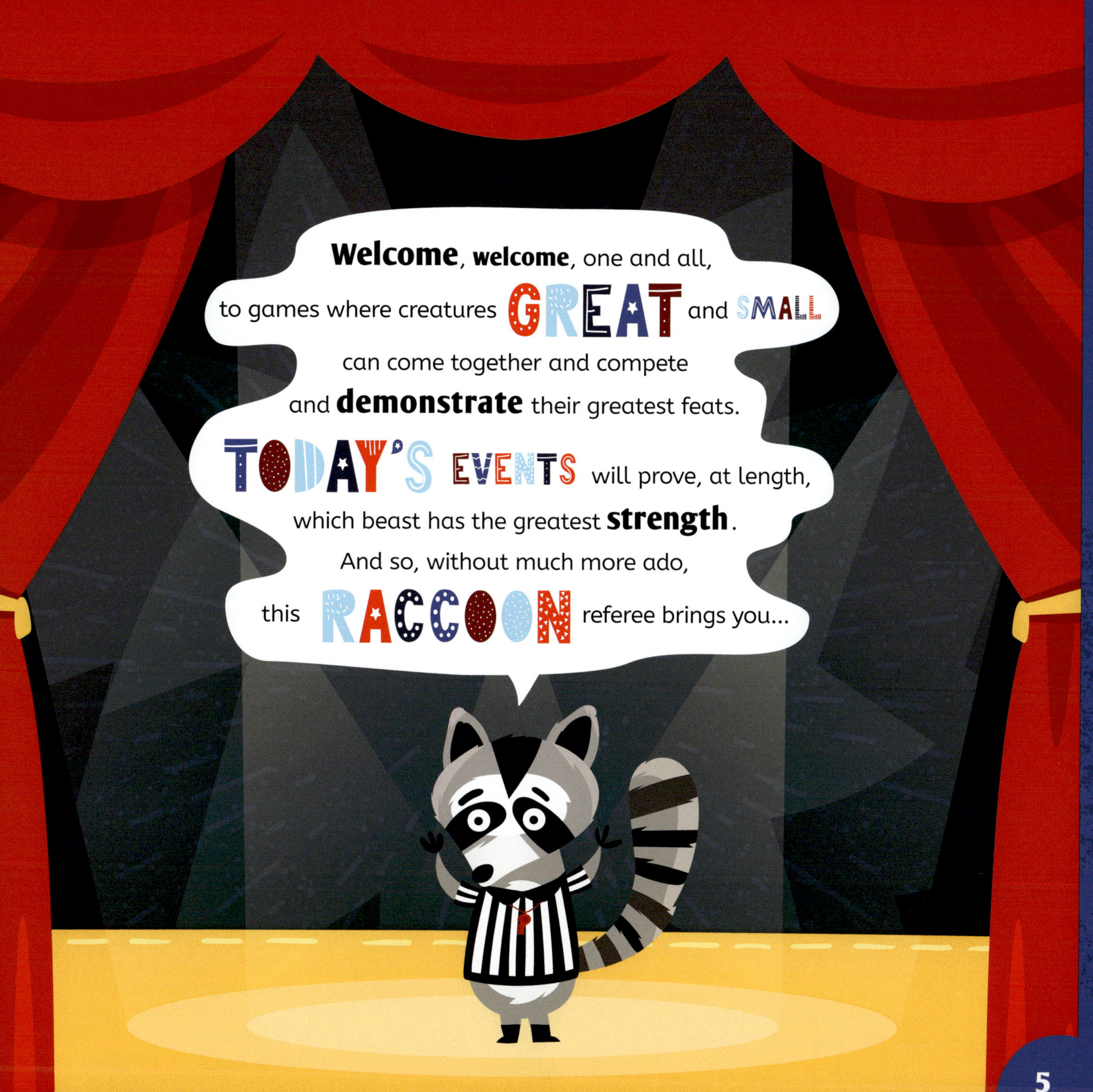
Welcome, welcome, one and all,
to games where creatures GREAT and SMALL
can come together and compete
and demonstrate their greatest feats.
TODAY'S EVENTS will prove, at length,
which beast has the greatest strength.
And so, without much more ado,
this RACCOON referee brings you...

# THE CONTENDERS

Let's find out some facts and figures about today's contenders!

**Dung Beetle**
Smelly but Strong

**Length:** Up to 0.4 inch (10 mm)

**Weight:** around 52 milligrams (mg)

**Load:** 1,150 x its weight!

**Leafcutter Ant**
The Mighty Bite

**Length:** Up to 0.6 inch (15 mm)

**Weight:** Up to 2 mg

**Load:** 50x its weight!

**Musk Ox**
The Arctic Avenger

**Height:** Up to 5 feet (1.5 m)

**Weight:** Up to 880 pounds (400 kg)

**Pull:** Up to 1,320 pounds (600 kg)

**Silverback Gorilla**
King of the Apes

**Height:** Up to 6 feet (1.8 m)

**Weight:** Up to 430 pounds (195 kg)

**Lift:** Up to 1,800 pounds (815 kg)

**Grizzly Bear**
The Ferocious Furball

**Height:** 6.5 feet (2 m) standing

**Weight:** 880 pounds (400 kg)

**Lift:** 880–1,100 pounds (400–500 kg)

**African Elephant**
The Gentle Giant

**Height:** 11 feet (3.3 m)

**Weight:** 13,230 pounds (6,000 kg)

**Lift:** 19,840 pounds (9,000 kg)

# SILVERBACK VS.

Rrrrrrround Onnnne!

ARGH!

Weighing in for the apes is the silverback gorilla. This Central African **primate** is a **herbivore**, but don't let that fool you; this mighty **mammal** is the biggest primate on the planet!

**Nickname:**
King of the Apes

**Super Strength:**
The gorilla's bite is twice as strong as a shark's.

# GRIZZLY BEAR

All the way from the North American **continent**, next up is the grizzly bear. This awesome **omnivore** has an incredible sense of smell, and can eat up to 90 pounds (40 kg) of food in a single day!

**Nickname:**
Ferocious Furball

**Super Strength:**
The grizzly's powerful claws can grow to 6 inches (15 cm) long!

GRRR!

**A few male grizzly bears have been recorded at 10 feet (3 m) tall and over 1,500 pounds (680 kg)!**

# THE TREE TRUNK LIFT

To find out who's the strongest, each **contender** must lift the heaviest tree trunk they can. Whoever lifts the heaviest is the winner!

**First up:** the silverback gorilla.

**That's more than four times the gorilla's body weight!**

**Gorilla:** 430 pounds (195 kg)

**Tree Trunk:** 1,800 pounds (815 kg)

Now for our **second contender:** the grizzly bear. Can he beat that?

**Bear:** 880 pounds (400 kg)

**Tree Trunk:** 1,100 pounds (500 kg)

# DUNG BEETLE VS.

SQUEAK!

Causing a stink in the beetle world, it's the dung beetle! Don't be put off by his smelly supper (he eats poop!) – this boss bug can move mountains.

**Nickname:**
Smelly but Strong

**Super Strength:**
The strongest dung beetle is called *Onthophagus taurus* (say: On-tho-FAY-gus TOR-us).

# LEAFCUTTER ANT

She might be little, but she's a big deal in the ant world. Leafcutter ants spend their days collecting leaf pieces, on which they grow a fungus to eat. This little farmer works hard!

**Nickname:**
The Mighty Bite

**Super Strength:**
Soldier leafcutter bites are so strong they can be used as staples to close open cuts!

**Leafcutter ants have special jobs. These include collecting food, protecting the colony, or even taking out the garbage!**

SNAP! SNAP!

# THE STRONG-BUG CIRCUS

Welcome to the strong-bug circus! Prepare to be amazed as the animal kingdom's smallest members show off their great strength!

**First up:** the dung beetle.

30,000 mg

30,000 mg

**That's like lifting more than 1,150 beetles!**

**Beetle:** 52 mg

**Weights:** 30,000 mg

**Total:** 60,000 mg

Our **second** contender, the leafcutter ant, is showing off her super strength.

**Ant:** 2 mg

**Weights:** 50 mg

**Total:** 100 mg

50 mg

50 mg

**That's as much as lifting 50 ants, using only her jaws!**

# AFRICAN ELEPHANT

This gentle giant leaves others in the shade! The African bush elephant is the largest land mammal on Earth! This hefty herbivore might seem kind and caring, but he's strong too!

**Nickname:**
The Gentle Giant

**Super Strength:**
A large male elephant can lift 660 pounds (300 kg) with just his trunk!

# VS. MUSK OX

He's heavy! He's hairy! He's an Ice Age animal who walked the Earth with the woolly mammoth, and still roams the **tundra** today. He might be smelly, but he's super strong!

**Nickname:**
The Arctic Avenger

**Super Strength:**
Can use its hooves to break Arctic ice to get to the water.

**What's that smell? Musk oxen make a scent, called musk, to mark their territory.**

BRRRGH!

# THE TUG-OF-WAR

Two heavyweight herbivores are face to face, but which one will pull their weight in the tug-of-war?

**Elephant Statistics**

**Weight:** 13,230 pounds (6,000 kg)

**Pull Force:** 19,840 pounds (9,000 kg)

**Musk Ox Statistics**

**Weight:** 880 pounds (400 kg)

**Pull Force:** 1,320 pounds (600 kg)

Round three goes to the **African elephant!**

**Although the ox can pull more than its own weight, the elephant is just too strong!**

# HALL OF FAME

**Green Anaconda**
Largest and heaviest snake in the world.

**Length:** Around 29.5 feet (9 m)

**Weight:** 500 pounds (227 kg)

**Strength:** Squeezes its prey to death

**Harpy Eagle**
World's largest and strongest bird of prey.

**Height:** 3 feet (0.9 m) tall

**Wingspan:** 6.5 feet (2 m)

**Strength:** Can fly with prey

**Shire Horse**
One of the strongest horse breeds.

**Height:** 6 feet (1.8 m) at shoulder

**Weight:** Around 2,200 pounds (1,000 kg)

**Strength:** Can pull twice its own weight

**Siberian Tiger**
The largest and strongest of the tigers.

**Length:** Around 11 feet (3.3 m)

**Weight:** Up to 800 pounds (360 kg)

**Strength:** Can pull twice its own weight

You've seen which beasts are incredibly strong;
now take our quiz – it won't take you long!

## Questions

1. How much does an African bush elephant weigh?
2. How many times its own body weight can a dung beetle pull?
3. Why does the musk ox smell?
4. What do leafcutter ants eat?
5. Is a silverback gorilla a carnivore or a herbivore?
6. How long can a grizzly bear's claws grow?

# ACTIVITY

Monkey bars are great for building strong arms – just like a gorilla!

Gymnastics are a great way to build strength in your whole body.

Get strong teeth like the leafcutter ant by brushing twice a day!

Answers from page 22: 1. 13,230 pounds. 2. Up to 1,150 times its own weight. 3. They make a scent to mark their territory. 4. Fungus, which they farm. 5. A herbivore. 6. 6 inches.

## GLOSSARY

**contender** someone who competes for a prize

**continent** a large area of land, often made up of several countries

**herbivore** an animal that eats only plants

**mammal** an animal that has warm blood, a backbone, and produces milk

**omnivore** an animal that eats plants and other animals

**primate** animals including humans, monkeys, and apes

**tundra** a cold area where trees do not grow